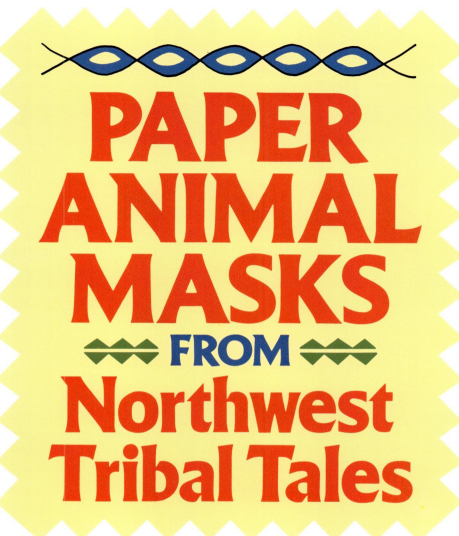

PAPER ANIMAL MASKS

FROM

Northwest Tribal Tales

◀ Nancy Lyn Rudolph ▶

Sterling Publishing Co., Inc. New York

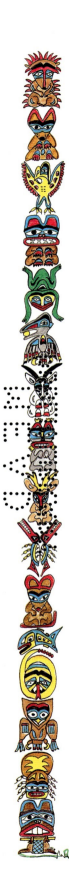

Edited by Jeanette Green

Library of Congress Cataloging-in-Publication Data

Rudolph, Nancy Lyn.
    Paper animal masks from northwest tribal tales / by Nancy Lyn
Rudolph.
       p.   cm.
    Includes index.
    ISBN 0-8069-4383-1
    1. Indians of North America—Northwest Coast of North America—
Folklore.   2. Indians of North America—Northwest, Pacific—
Folklore.   3. Mask making—Juvenile literature.   4. Indian masks—
Northwest Coast of North America—Juvenile literature.   5. Indian
masks—Northwest, Pacific—Juvenile literature.   I. Title.
E78.N78R85   1996
398.2′089970795—dc20   95-39222

1   3   5   7   9   10   8   6   4   2

Published by Sterling Publishing Company, Inc.
387 Park Avenue South, New York, N.Y. 10016
© 1996 by Nancy Lyn Rudolph
Distributed in Canada by Sterling Publishing
% Canadian Manda Group, One Atlantic Avenue, Suite 105
Toronto, Ontario, Canada M6K 3E7
Distributed in Great Britain and Europe by Cassell PLC
Wellington House, l25 Strand, London WC2R 0BB, England
Distributed in Australia by Capricorn Link (Australia) Pty Ltd.
P.O. Box 6651, Baulkham Hills, Business Centre, NSW 2153, Australia
Printed in Hong Kong
All rights reserved

Sterling ISBN 0-8069-4383-1

Acknowledgments

The children in masks and the statue of Chief Seattle were photographed by **Tony Blanchett. Joy Spurr** photographed all the animals found in the wild, except for the coyote and salmon, which were photographed by **Spirit Wind Wildlife Photography.**

These animal tales have many versions and variations, which can be found in the folktale sources of your library. The Spider tale used here, however, relies on the version by Mourning Dove, "Why Spider Has Long Legs," courtesy of Heister Dean Guie, Ed. *Coyote Stories.* Lincoln: University of Nebraska Press, 1990, pp. 129–131.

Ted Perry's poem on p. 4, inspired by Chief Seattle, is reproduced by permission from Eli Gifford and Michael R. Cook, Eds. *How Can One Sell the Air?* Summertown, Tenn.: Book Publishing Co., 1992.

CONTENTS

TONY BLANCHETT

CHIEF SEATTLE

"What is man without the beast?
Even the earthworm keeps the earth soft
for man to walk upon.
If all the beasts were gone, men would
die from great loneliness.
For whatever happens to the beasts, happens to man
for we are all of one breath."

Ted Perry, inspired by Chief Seattle's 1854 speech

PREFACE

· · · · · · · · · · · ·

The spirits of our ancestors are with us today. However, the challenge in this day and age is to allow ourselves the time to communicate with them.

It has been said by our old ones that the spiritual beings represented in our ancestral masks and stories have been here since long before humankind. Thus, our association with these spiritual forces is rooted in respect for the natural environment which the Creator of us all has provided. Animal stories, art and activities, woven into daily life, incorporate that respect and teach about our culture and customs.

A long time ago, myths, legends, stories, songs and dances were shared with young children during the evening hours by firelight. The darkness made it more difficult to be distracted by the tools and toys of everyday life, and the firelight focused attention and brought to mind something less familiar and more full of possibilities than daylight. The separation between the human and animal worlds became less clear.

This collection of ancient animal stories from northwestern North America delights and instructs with dignity and gentle humor. Often working at several levels, the stories teach and entertain, but all speak to people of every age. In simple terms, Bear's tale shows a bond between spiritual, animal and human realms; Eagle's story speaks of equality and generosity; and Porcupine's wisdom prevails over self-centered foolishness.

Although native people carved wooden masks from cedar, the paper mask-making activities and illustrations here serve as modern-day interpretations of the ancient arts of the people of the Northwest coast. They reinforce the stories' messages connecting natural and spiritual worlds, and provide children an enjoyable way to become acquainted with and gain an interest in our people's traditions and crafts.

As you read the stories, make the animal masks, and think about the old ways, we hope you will gain a better understanding of what they represented to the ancestors of the native peoples of this region. Whether you use this book during the daytime or in the evening, we hope that these mask activities and animal stories will add something to the way you live and guide you to an appreciation of the spiritual forces of nature.

Henry Kwi-Tlum-Kadim Gobin
Cultural Resources Manager

Tulalip Tribes of Washington

Northwest Tribes
North Pacific Coast, Plateau, and California Cultures

ALASKA

CANADA

Tlingit

ROCKY MOUNTAINS

COASTAL MOUNTAINS

Tsimshian

NORTH PACIFIC COAST

Kutenai

PUGET SOUND

Tulalip

Sanpoil

Colville

CASCADE MOUNTAINS

Quileute

Yakima

PLATEAU

Klickitat

Chehalis

Nez Perce

PACIFIC OCEAN

Modoc

UNITED STATES

CALIFORNIA

THE ANIMAL PEOPLE

People have made masks for thousands of years. Some were designed for practical uses, such as a disguise for a hunter, while others were created for use in storytelling, teaching, or special celebrations. Many people believed wearing a mask or costume actually caused things to happen—the person hidden inside could take on the special features or skills of whatever the mask or costume portrayed.

Although representations of the sun, moon, and imaginary creatures were common, animals provided a major theme in the crafts and culture of early North Americans. These tribes lived close to nature and held their environment in high regard, especially valuing the animals which supplied food, clothing, and shelter through their flesh, skins, and fur. Even their bones and teeth were fashioned into tools and ornaments.

The first Americans did not write their history; they passed information from one generation to the next through storytelling (oral tradition). As in other cultures around the world, many *legends* were loosely based upon history, and *myths* explained religious beliefs or customs. Although *folktales* were also used in crafts, dance, and celebrations, creation stories and other tales of transformation served the culture in important ways. These stories explained matters beyond people's understanding, and many tales featuring animals taught basic truths about honesty, courage, and sharing, as well as other qualities valued by the culture and the specific community.

In the mythology of many early North American tribes, all things had an inner spirit which made them behave in a certain way. The greatest spirits lived in the Sky World or on the tops of the highest mountains, and these supernatural beings created the earth, helped by animal people. The animal people of those days looked much like animals today, but they talked, thought, walked, and acted much like humans. Some also had special powers, especially Raven on the North Pacific Coast and Coyote in the East and Southwest. Much later, ordinary people lived on the earth with the creatures we now know.

Animals, then, were seen as ancestors. Clans often had a mythological founder, usually animal. The totem poles of the ranked societies of the North Pacific Coast indicated the hierarchy of the clan(s) and the totem animal(s).

Animal masks permitted the wearer to transform himself into an animal and enter, temporarily, into the spirit world. These masks were highly valued as personal possessions. And mask wearing was a privilege.

The animal masks in this book were inspired by Northwest tribes that inhabited what are today the northwestern United States, western Canada, and Alaska. The animal tales are adapted from those commonly told by tribes of the North Pacific Coast, Plateau, and California cultures. They include creation stories, many tales of transformation, tales from trickster cycles, and an animal husband tale. These animal masks and tales celebrate the richness of the traditions of the Tlingit, Tsimshian, Tulalip, Sanpoil, Kutenai, Quileute, Chehelais, Colville, Yakima, Klicki-tat, Nez Perce, Modoc, and other tribes. The traditions of making and wearing animal masks and storytelling about animals continue today.

Materials

All masks in this book are constructed from 9×12-inch sheets of medium-weight construction paper, folded or cut in different ways. Special colors or supplies for individual masks are listed under ''Supplies'' with each project. Besides construction paper, you'll need a stapler, transparent tape or glue, scissors, 1×3-inch self-adhesive labels, a hole punch, yarn, and crayons or felt-tip markers.

About Authenticity

The tales in this book were adapted from some of the many animal tales of the first Americans who lived in what are now the northwestern United States and western Canada. The animal drawings are not meant to authentically represent native art, and the paper animal masks are not direct replications of those used by these cultures.

ANIMAL TALES & MASKS

JOY SPURR

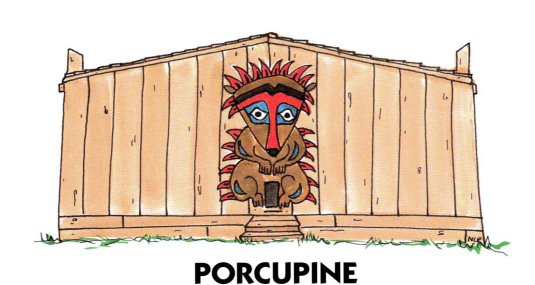

PORCUPINE

Grizzly Bear invited all the animals to a meeting. Many were being killed by hunters. He said, "Let's ask the Great Spirit to make winters colder and longer to keep the hunters inside their houses and out of the forests." The big animals liked the idea; the little animals didn't.

Porcupine stood up to speak. "You big animals wear thick fur that keeps you warm all winter, but what about the smallest among us? Some have no fur at all. They will die in the cold. We should keep things as they are.

"No," said Cougar, Elk, and Wolf. "We need more winter. The little people don't count."

Porcupine spoke again. "If the winters become colder and longer, all the plants will freeze and die, too. There won't be berries, leaves, and grasses for you to eat in the spring and summer." Porcupine was so angry at the big animals' foolish idea that he bit off his own thumb and spit it out in front of everyone!

The animals thought about Porcupine's words. "Porcupine is wise," they agreed. "Let's ask for six months of winter and six months of summer. When it's coldest, the big animals can hide in dens so that hunters won't find them." They made Porcupine Chief of the Little Animals and asked him to stay out all winter to check on the other small animals. He never got his thumb back, though, and to this day Porcupine has only four fingers on his hand.

Adapted from a Tsimshian tale

MAKE A PORCUPINE MASK

TONY BLANCHETT

Supplies

- 2½ sheets of 9×12-inch brown construction paper
- 1½×1½-inch scrap of black paper for nose

3. Cut out the eyeholes from both thicknesses, making them about two fingers (1¼ inches) wide.

TOP QUILLS

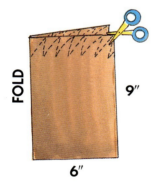

FOLD

9″

6″

1. Fold a 9×12-inch sheet of brown construction paper in half. Cut a jagged edge at the top with scissors.

2. Mark the position of the eyeholes about halfway down from the top edge and one finger in from the fold.

4. For Porcupine's quills, fold a second sheet of brown paper in half as in step 1. Cut the paper into four strips (each about 2×12 inches). Keeping a strip folded in half, cut a jagged edge on one long

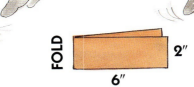

FOLD 2"

6"

side. Repeat with two of the other strips. Save one uncut strip for step 8.

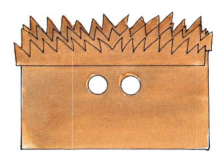

5. Open out the head piece. Lay one strip across the top of Porcupine's head below the top jagged edge, keeping the spines pointing up. Staple or glue them in place. Repeat with a second strip.

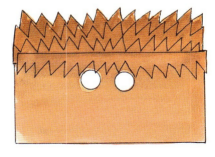

6. For a third strip, turn spines down toward the face.

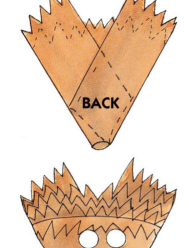

BACK

FRONT

7. Bend the head piece into a pointed cone shape, leaving a small mouth opening at one end. The other end should be open wide enough to fit over a person's face. Attach inside corners with staples.

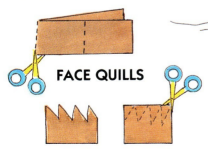

FACE QUILLS

8. Cut the fourth 2×12-inch strip into four pieces. Make one long side jagged

on two of the pieces. Attach to the sides of the face, spines pointing in.

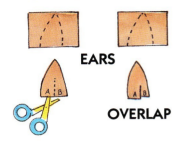

EARS

OVERLAP

9. Cut two small ears from the other two pieces. Cut to center and overlap edges A and B to make ears stand out. Attach the ears to the top sides of the head with staples or glue. Cut the nose from the small black piece and attach. Draw a mouth with crayon or a marker.

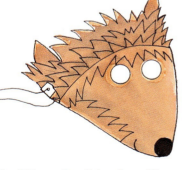

10. Wrap 1×3-inch self-adhesive label around the side of the mask at the bottom corners. Punch holes for ties and attach 12-inch pieces of yarn or string.

13

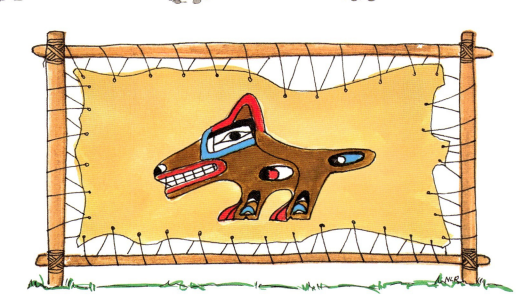

COYOTE

Coyote did not like his name. He wanted to be called Eagle or Salmon or Grizzly Bear. When the Great Spirit announced he would give names to all the animals at dawn, Coyote planned to be first in line.

His friends teased him, saying, "No one wants to be called Coyote. You are stuck with that name." Although he tried hard to stay awake that night, Coyote's eyelids grew too heavy to stay open. Awakening with the full sun in his face, he ran to the Great Spirit's lodge, only to discover that all the other animals had arrived ahead of him. The Great Spirit had named Eagle, Chief of Birds; Grizzly Bear, Chief of Land Animals; and Salmon, Chief of the Sea. Only the name Coyote remained.

Coyote started to turn away, his ears drooping in disappointment, when the Great Spirit called to him. "Coyote," he said, "I have another task for you. You will not be called Eagle or Grizzly Bear or Salmon, but you will have a special power not given to any other animal. You will be Helper of Others."

Adapted from a Colville tale

MAKE A COYOTE MASK

TONY BLANCHETT

Supplies

- sheet of 9×12-inch tan construction paper
- sheet of 6×6-inch brown construction paper to make eyebrows and ears
- piece of 1½×1½-inch black paper for nose

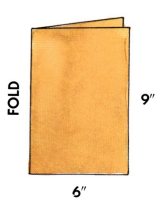

FOLD

9"

6"

1. Fold a 9×12-inch sheet of tan construction paper in half.

2. Measure three fingers down from top edge and one finger in from fold to mark the position of eyeholes.

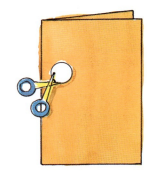

3. Cut out eyeholes from both thicknesses, making them about two fingers (1¼ inches) wide.

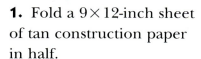

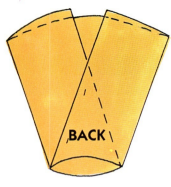

BACK

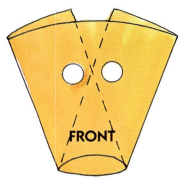

FRONT

4. Open out, then bend the sheet into a loose cone, attaching the inside corners with staples.

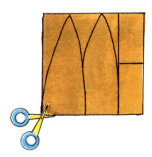

5. Cut out ears and eyebrows from brown construction paper.

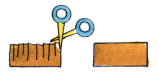

EYEBROWS

6. Use scissors to fringe the eyebrows to give them a hairy look.

EARS

OVERLAP

7. Slit ears at the base and overlap edges to make them stand out.

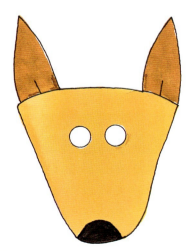

8. Attach ears at the top of the head, and add a construction paper nose.

9. Attach eyebrows above the eyes, and draw a mouth with a black crayon or marker.

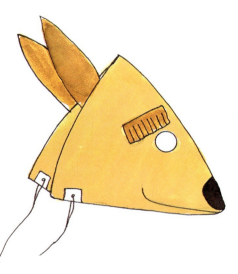

10. Wrap 1 × 3-inch self-adhesive label around the outside and inside back corners. Punch holes for ties and attach a 12-inch piece of yarn or string to each.

17

JOY SPURR

EAGLE

Long ago, before the birds wore colored feathers, the Animal People on the beach watched a strange and colorful bird fly over the sea. Many strong young men tried to catch it but could not. When two young children of Chief Eagle announced they had a plan that might succeed, they were laughed at by the men of the village because they were girls.

Ignoring the jokes and hidden in trees behind the village, the girls worked secretly. At dawn one day, they paddled a canoe far out to sea and easily captured the special creature in the trap they had built.

When they showed the treasured creature to their proud and delighted father, Chief Eagle invited all the animals from neighboring villages to a celebration. At the party, the Eagle girls gave each visiting bird a different colored feather taken from the beautiful bird, until all the birds received the colors they wear today.

Adapted from a Quileute tale

MAKE AN EAGLE MASK

TONY BLANCHETT

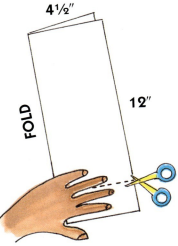

4½″

FOLD

12″

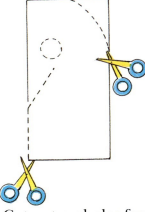

1. Fold a 9×12-inch sheet of white construction paper in half. Measure about two fingers from bottom edge, and cut off and save this strip.

2. Measure three fingers down from the top edge and one finger in from the fold to mark the position of the eyeholes.

3. Cut out eyeholes from both thicknesses, making them about two fingers (1¼ inches) wide. Cut off corners at the top to make a rounded head. From the bottom edge, cut a slit along the fold, then an-

20

other slit angled in from the fold to make a beak.

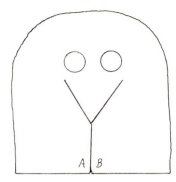

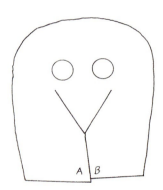

4. Open out. Overlap bottom edges A and B and staple, making the beak stand out from the face.

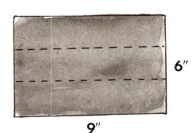

6"

9"

5. Cut the half sheet of black construction paper into three 9×2-inch strips.

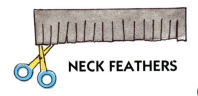

NECK FEATHERS

Fringe with scissors to give a feathery look.

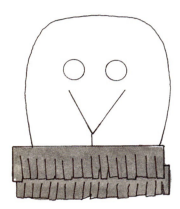

6. Attach strips to the bottom of the face with staples, tape, or glue. Attach the bottom row first, then overlap other rows. Trim edges to be even with the sides of the mask.

BEAK

7. Cut a beak from a 3×3-inch square of yellow construction paper. Fold in half on the diagonal. Then cut a curved piece from one edge. Staple or tape

the yellow beak to the white "under-beak," placing curved sides down.

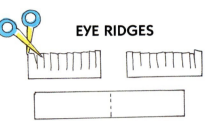

EYE RIDGES

8. Using the white strip saved from step 1, cut into two pieces. Fringe with scissors as in step 5 to give a feathery look and attach to the face above the eyes for eye ridges.

9. Wrap a 1×3-inch self-adhesive label around the outside and inside at eye level. Punch holes for ties and attach 12-inch pieces of yarn or string.

JOY SPURR

BEAR

A chill gripped the Sky World, home of the Great Spirit; so, he moved his household to a mountaintop where sunshine warmed the land. One day, after gathering flowers in a meadow, his young daughter wandered into the mountain's great forests and became lost. A family of bears, talking and walking upon two legs as they did in those days, took her home. The bears did not tell the Great Spirit they had found his missing daughter. When this special spirit girl grew up, she married a bear, and their children, neither animals nor spirits, became the first people.

Angered to see the new creatures he did not create, the Great Spirit scattered the humans to live in all parts of the world. To the animals he said, "Forevermore, all bears must walk on four legs, never again speak, and remain hidden in the forests."

Adapted from a Modoc creation story

23

MAKE A BEAR MASK

TONY BLANCHETT

Supplies

- sheet of 9×12-inch brown construction paper
- 3 pieces of 3×3-inch brown paper for nose and ears, cut from bottom of sheet

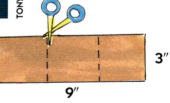

3″

9″

2. Cut off a strip about four fingers wide from bottom edge. Cut the strip into three squares, each about 3×3 inches.

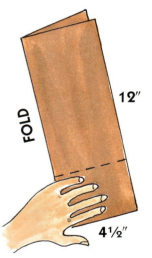

12″

FOLD

4½″

1. Fold a 9×12-inch sheet of brown construction paper in half.

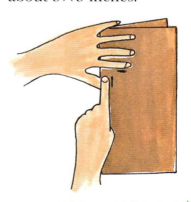

3. Mark the position of the eyeholes, using three fingers to measure down from the top edge and one finger in from fold.

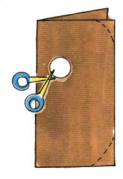

4. Cut out eyeholes from both thicknesses, making them about two fingers (1¼ inches) wide. Cut the top and bottom outside corners off to make the head rounded.

NOSE

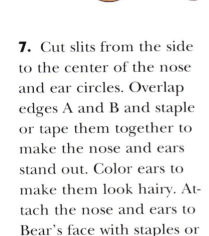

EARS

FRINGE

5. Open out and color the sides of the face with black or dark brown crayon or a marker to give a hairy look. Add eyebrows.

NOSE

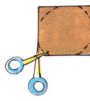

EARS

6. For Bear's nose, cut a circle from one of the small brown pieces of construction paper. Cut circles for ears from the other two pieces of brown paper.

7. Cut slits from the side to the center of the nose and ear circles. Overlap edges A and B and staple or tape them together to make the nose and ears stand out. Color ears to make them look hairy. Attach the nose and ears to Bear's face with staples or tape.

NOSE

OVERLAP

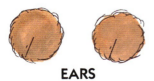

EARS

8. Add a mouth and whisker spots with a crayon or marker. Cut a slit from the bottom edge to nose and overlap edges A and B to make the face stand out.

9. Wrap 1 × 3-inch self-adhesive label around side of mask. Punch holes for ties and attach 12-inch pieces of yarn or string.

JOY SPURR

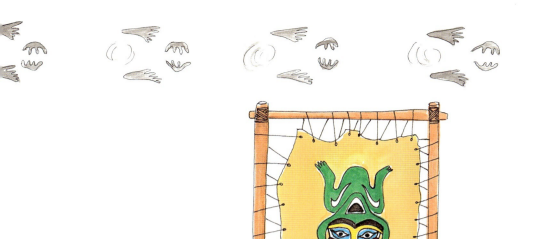

FROG

Frog and Antelope lived in neighboring villages. Whenever footraces were held, Antelope always won. Antelope's reputation grew as more and more animals came from far away to challenge him. But none was as quick. He began to think of himself as the king of runners, boasting, "No one can beat me."

Frog, tired of hearing Antelope brag, thought of a plan to teach him a lesson. He visited the great speedster to ask him if he wanted to race. Antelope laughed out loud, thinking, "I will easily outrun this squatty Frog," They agreed upon a date and time for the big event.

Frog went home to confer with his friends and family. He asked all the frogs to lie down a little distance apart in the high grass along the racetrack and stay hidden. "When the race starts," he said, "you must each take a turn running."

The race began and Antelope looked at the small challenger hopping along at his side. Slowing his pace, he thought, "No need to hurry today." As Antelope poked along, his head high, Frog's cousin took over for Frog, then another cousin took his place, then the third, fourth, and fifth, and others after them. To his shock, Antelope noticed he had fallen behind, but even as he ran faster, Frog seemed to stay ahead. Antelope sped up, his long legs flying over the hard ground, but too late. Frog hopped over the finish line first.

Adapted from a Kutenai folktale

MAKE A FROG MASK

TONY BLANCHETT

HEAD SHAPE

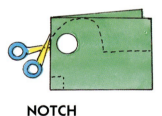

NOTCH

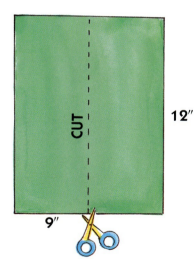

CUT

12″

9″

1. Cut a 9×12-inch sheet of green construction paper in half.

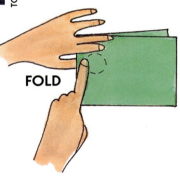

FOLD

2. For the face, fold one piece in half again. Mark the position of the eyeholes using two fingers to measure down from the top edge and one finger in from the fold.

3. Cut out eyeholes from both thicknesses, making them about two fingers (1¼ inches) wide. Cut a rounded shape for the top of the head, leaving the sides straight. Cut a notch at the lower corner of the fold.

TONGUE

4. Open out, adding spots and accenting the eyes and brows with black or brown crayon or a marker.

6. Completely flatten and fold over one open end with the folded piece about two fingers wide.

8. Cut a long, thin strip from pink construction paper, and fold back and forth like a fan for a tongue. Attach the tongue inside the mouth.

MOUTH

5. For the mouth, roll the second half sheet of green construction paper into a flat cylinder and staple or tape the ends together.

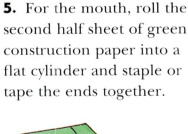

7. Attach the flattened, folded end to the frog face below the eyes. Add nostrils with crayon or a marker.

9. Wrap a 1 × 3-inch self-adhesive label around the side of the mask. Punch holes for ties and attach 12-inch pieces of yarn or string.

JOY SPURR

RAVEN

Raven, a strong and handsome white bird, saw that the animal people were unhappy. He knew an evil Sky Spirit had taken the sun, moon, stars, fresh water, and fire from the people and hidden them in a box in his lodge.

"Raven, you are good and can do many things," the villagers cried. "We are thirsty and live in cold and darkness. Will you find the light, water, and fire in the Sky World and bring them back to us?"

Raven flew up to the Sky World and slipped, unnoticed, into the Sky Spirit's lodge. He opened the box holding the sun, moon, stars, and water and put them on his back. With his beak, he grasped a flaming stick from the fire pit. Soaring outside, he hung the sun, moon, and stars in the sky and dropped the water over the land.

Before he could return fire to the waiting villagers, the dark smoke from the burning torch in his beak blew back over him and turned his feathers black. Ever since, people have shared the sun, moon, stars, fire, and fresh water. And Raven has been a black bird.

Adapted from a story told by several Puget Sound tribes

MAKE A RAVEN MASK

Supplies

- sheet of 9×12-inch black construction paper
- half sheet of 9×12-inch yellow construction paper, cut to 4½×12″
- a few dark feathers, if available

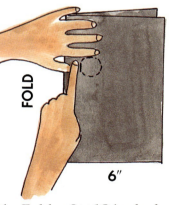

FOLD

9″

6″

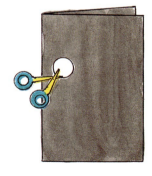

BACK

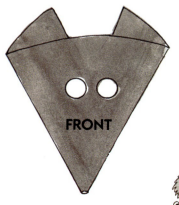

FRONT

1. Fold a 9×12-inch sheet of black construction paper in half. Mark the position of the eyeholes using three fingers to measure down from the top edge and one finger in from the fold.

2. Cut out eyeholes from both thicknesses, making them about two fingers (1¼ inches) wide.

TONY BLANCHETT

3. Open out, then bend the sheet into a tight cone shape, sharply pointed at one end and open wide enough to fit over a person's face at the other. Attach inside corners with staples.

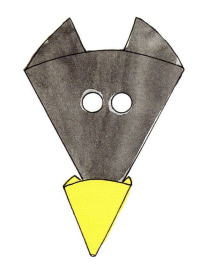

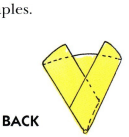

BACK

BEAK

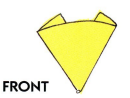

FRONT

4. For Raven's beak, bend the 4½ × 12-inch sheet of yellow construction paper into a tight cone to fit over the black cone.

5. Attach the cones together with staples or tape.

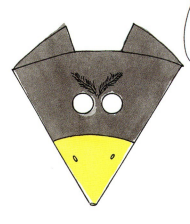

6. If available, add feathers to the face near the eyes. Add nostrils and a mouth with crayon or marker.

7. Wrap a 1 × 3-inch self-adhesive label around each side of mask. Punch holes for ties and attach 12-inch pieces of yarn or string.

JOY SPURR

MOUNTAIN GOAT

Long ago, when people hunted Mountain Goat, they killed more animals than they needed and left the flesh to rot on the ground. Mountain Goat's relatives became few, and many of their spirits were held captive in dry bones scattered in the rugged peaks. A young man spoke against this waste and cruelty. When he saw children tease a baby goat, he rescued the small creature and returned it to its craggy home.

One day, a visitor stopped at the village and invited everyone to a grand party at the foot of the mountain. To the kind young man he said, ''Do not join the others. Climb high into the mountains across the valley.'' The celebration grew loud as the people danced and ate. Suddenly, a goat with a single horn appeared on a rocky ledge. Kicking and pawing, the fearful animal created a landslide, burying the greedy and thoughtless villagers under snow and rock.

The young man looked for his new friend, but only a goat carrying a wool blanket stood nearby. When he put the blanket over his shoulders, he found he could leap from rock to rock and cross patches of snow with surefooted ease. He gathered the bones of animals hurt by children or needlessly slain by hunters and burned them to release their spirits. Because one person was kind, Mountain Goat and his people have lived free and wild among the peaks ever since.

Adapted from a Tsimshian tale

MAKE A MOUNTAIN GOAT MASK

TONY BLANCHETT

Supplies

- sheet of 9×12-inch white construction paper
- 2 pieces of 2×4-inch white paper for ears
- piece of 4×6-inch white paper for beard and "bangs"
- 2 pieces of 6×6-inch black construction paper for horns
- small piece of pink paper for tongue

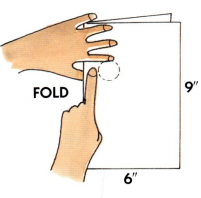

FOLD

9"

6"

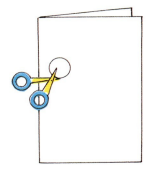

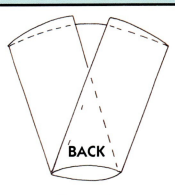

BACK

FRONT

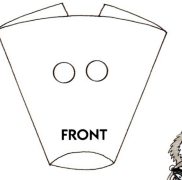

1. Fold a 9×12-inch sheet of white construction paper in half. Measure three fingers down from top edge and one finger in from the fold to mark the position of the eyeholes.

2. Cut out eyeholes from both thicknesses, making them about two fingers (1¼ inches) wide.

3. Open out, then bend the sheet into a loose cone, attaching inside corners with staples.

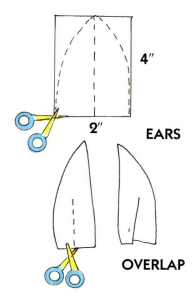

EARS

OVERLAP

4. Cut out ears from 2×4-inch pieces of white construction paper. Ears can be slit at the base to make them stand out.

HORNS

5. Starting at one corner, roll up 6×6-inch pieces of black construction paper to make two horns. Tape overlapped edges.

BANGS AND BEARD

6. Make the beard and bangs from a 4×6-inch piece of white construction paper cut in half. Use one half for the bangs and the other for the beard. Fringe with scissors to give a hairy look. Attach the beard to the chin and the bangs to the forehead with staples, tape, or glue. Add a tongue.

7. Attach horns at top center and ears at the top

sides of the head. Add a black construction-paper nose, and draw a mouth with black crayon or a marker.

8. Wrap a 1×3-inch self-adhesive label around the outside and inside the back corners. Punch holes for ties and attach 12-inch pieces of yarn or string.

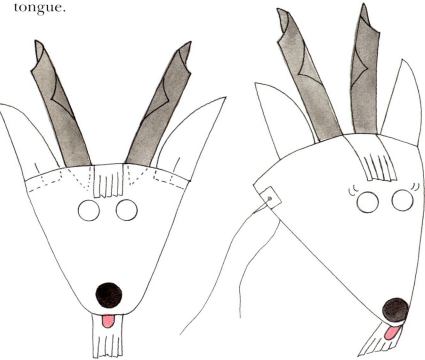

JOY SPURR

LYNX

Lynx made a camp in the rocks so he could keep an eye on Coyote. He watched when Coyote got up early and trotted off toward the lake. And he observed Coyote loping home, carrying something in a bag. Lynx saw him leave the next morning and return later in the day with another bulging sack.

Awakening from a nap, the smell of burning meat on the wind, Lynx leaped down from his lofty lookout and stealthily crept toward Coyote's camp. Getting closer, he could see duck meat roasting on the fire and Coyote fast asleep. Remembering his empty stomach, Lynx took the food. As a joke, he pulled on Coyote's nose making his face longer; then he tugged on his tail, stretching it out, also.

Coyote awoke as Lynx sprinted off. When Coyote saw what had happened, he went to Lynx's camp. Finding Lynx napping, Coyote gathered up the leftover duck meat. He grabbed Lynx's tail and shoved it in, making it stubby, and took Lynx's face and pushed it in, flattening his nose. This is why Coyote has a long face and long tail, and Lynx has a short face and short tail.

Adapted from a Kutenai transformation tale

MAKE A LYNX MASK

TONY BLANCHETT

Supplies

- sheet of 9×12-inch gray or tan construction paper
- small piece of white paper for teeth
- small piece of pink paper for tongue
- 2 white pipe cleaners, about 6 inches long, for whiskers (optional)

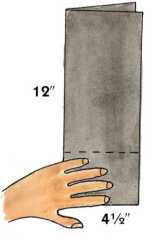

12″

4½″

1. Fold a 9×12-inch sheet of gray or tan construction paper in half. Measuring with four fingers, cut a strip about 3 inches wide off the bottom.

2. Mark the position of the eyeholes using three fingers to measure down from the top edge and one finger in from the edge. Cut out the eyeholes from both thicknesses, making them about two fingers (1¼ inches) wide. Round the corners of the head.

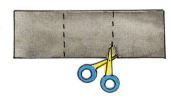

3. Cut the strip saved from step 1 into three parts for the ears and nose.

4. Cut ears from two parts of the strip.

40

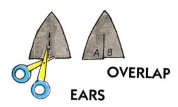

OVERLAP EARS

Cut a slit at the bottom of the ears. Overlap edges A and B slightly, and tape or staple them together to make the ears stand out.

6. Fold side pieces into each side center fold. Press the top edge together slightly.

teeth and a tongue. Draw whiskers below the nose or poke white pipe cleaners through the face below the nose. Use a black crayon or marker to give the face and ears a hairy look. Spots or other fur colors can be added with yellow, brown, black, or white crayons.

Attach the ears to the top of the head near the corners.

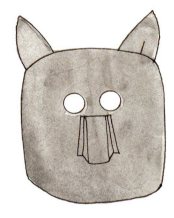

7. Flatten and attach the top edge of the nose to the face between the eyes. Leave the bottom end of the nose open, but attach sides, allowing the center flattened area to stand out.

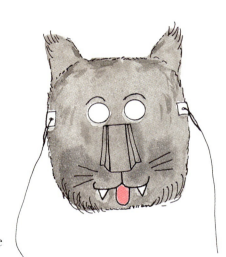

NOSE

5. For Lynx's nose, fold the last 3×3-inch part saved from step 1 into thirds.

8. Add a mouth with crayon or a marker. Using white and pink scraps of paper, make and attach

9. Wrap a 1×3-inch self-adhesive label around each side of the mask at eye level. Punch holes for ties and attach 12-inch pieces of yarn or string.

JOY SPURR

DEER

In the old days, Deer had a silky fur coat. He looked handsome and stayed warm inside the ample, plush fur, but he often caught long strands of his beautiful coat on bark and jagged rocks in the high country where he lived. He would say to himself, "This pretty fur is too much trouble. I wish I had short hair. Then, I could slip through the trees quickly and easily. Never again would I hear the *rrrip* of fur snagged on brush or feel the pain of long hair torn from my skin."

Rabbit lived in the lowlands where sagebrush grew and no forest provided warmth and shelter. Sometimes, on cold nights, he could feel the chill through his short hairy coat. Rabbit thought, "I wish I had thicker fur; then I would stay warm all winter."

One summer day, Deer saw Rabbit sunning himself by the river, his short-haired coat drying on a rock nearby. Quietly, Deer took off his own fur coat and put it beside Rabbit's. He slipped into the small, coarse-haired coat, stretching it to fit tightly over his bigger body. "Rabbit," Deer said, "I will wear your coat back to the mountains. You can have my woolly fur coat." Ever since, Rabbit has kept snug and warm in Deer's old roomy fur, and Deer has moved freely through the forest without tearing or catching his short hair on brush or trees.

Adapted from a Yakima tale

MAKE A DEER MASK

TONY BLANCHETT

Supplies

- sheet of 9×12-inch brown construction paper
- quarter sheet of 9×12-inch brown paper for ears
- 2 sheets of 9×12-inch tan construction paper for antlers
- piece of 2×2-inch black paper for nose

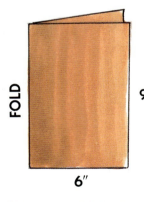

FOLD

9"

6"

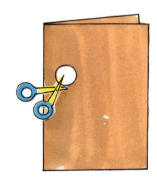

1. Fold a 9×12-inch sheet of brown construction paper in half.

2. Mark position of eyeholes using three fingers to measure down from the top edge and one finger in from the fold.

3. Cut out eyeholes from both thicknesses, making them about two fingers (1¼ inches) wide.

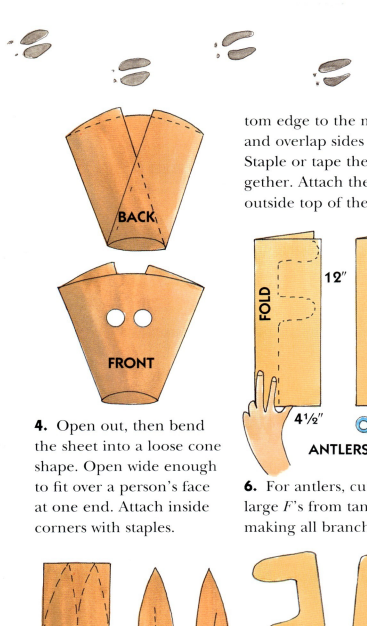

BACK

FRONT

4. Open out, then bend the sheet into a loose cone shape. Open wide enough to fit over a person's face at one end. Attach inside corners with staples.

EARS

OVERLAP

5. Cut out ears from the quarter sheet of brown paper. To make ears stand out, cut a slit from the bottom edge to the middle and overlap sides slightly. Staple or tape them together. Attach them at the outside top of the head.

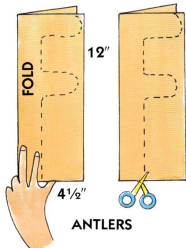

FOLD

12″

4½″

ANTLERS

6. For antlers, cut out two large *F*'s from tan paper, making all branches about two fingers wide. Round off corners. Glue or tape closed all open edges. Attach antlers between the ears on top of the head.

7. Add mouth and nose with crayon or marker, or cut a round nose from black paper and attach.

8. Wrap a 1 × 3-inch self-adhesive label around the back lower corners of the mask. Punch holes for ties and attach 12-inch pieces of yarn or string.

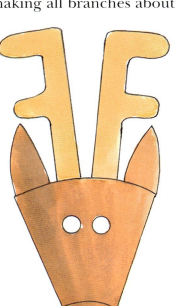

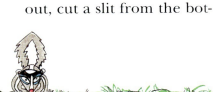

JOY SPURR

MOUSE

A princess lived with her family. One night, a handsome young man came to visit her. He changed himself into a mouse and entered the house through a knothole above the girl's bed. They fell in love and secretly married. When the princess's father learned of the marriage and that his daughter expected a baby, he ordered his family to put the princess in a box and send it down the river to the sea.

When the box washed up on the shore of a distant island, villagers opened it. To their surprise, mice spilled out and ran off in all directions. Then they saw the princess step out. She became part of the new villagers' community, married again, and had many children.

When the princess's children grew up, they asked their mother questions about her past. Paddling their canoes for many days, the young people searched for her old home. One day they stopped at a village of mice. "We're your mother's children, too!" the mice said. "Long ago, she married a mouse prince."

A celebration began. The villagers slept in the day, awoke at dusk, then danced until daybreak. The mice taught the newcomers to dance, too. When time came to return home, everyone gathered on the beach. The princess's children thanked the little people for teaching them how to dance. Chief Mouse gave a speech. He said, "Always treat mice well. Remember, all mice are of noble blood."

Adapted from a Tsimshian animal husband tale

MAKE A MOUSE MASK

TONY BLANCHETT

Supplies

- sheet of 9×12-inch brown construction paper
- two 3×3-inch squares of pink construction paper for ears
- 2 white pipe cleaners about 6 inches long
- scrap of white paper for teeth
- piece of 1×1-inch pink paper for nose

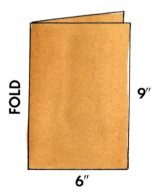

FOLD

9"

6"

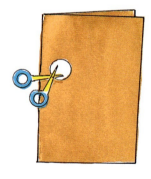

1. Fold a 9×12-inch sheet of brown construction paper in half.

2. Mark the position of the eyeholes using three fingers to measure down from the top edge and one finger in from the fold.

3. Cut out eyeholes from both thicknesses, making them about two fingers (1¼ inches) wide.

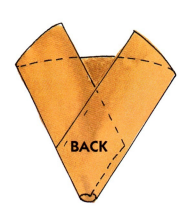

BACK

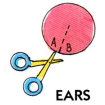

EARS

OVERLAP

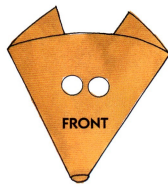

FRONT

5. Cut round ears from 3 ×3-inch pieces of pink paper. Cut a slit from the bottom edge to the center of the ear. Overlap edges A and B and staple or tape them to make the ears stand out.

from pink paper scrap. Cut two mouse teeth from white scrap and attach them inside the mouth with tape. Poke small holes through the face below the nose to attach pipe-cleaner whiskers.

4. Open out then bend the sheet into a tight cone shape that's pointed but not closed at one end, and open wide enough to fit over a person's face at the other. Attach the inside corners with staples.

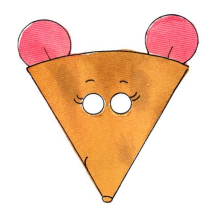

6. Attach ears to the top sides of the head with staples or tape. Draw a mouth, eyebrows, and eyelashes with crayon or marker.

7. Add a round nose drawn with crayon or cut

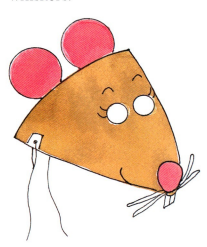

8. Wrap a 1×3-inch self-adhesive label around the side of the mask at the bottom corners. Punch holes for ties and attach 12-inch pieces of yarn or string.

EARS

49

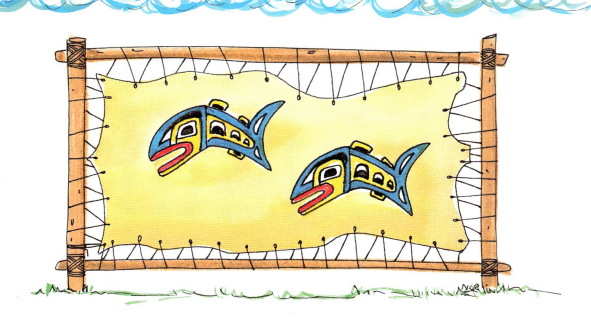

SALMON

Great numbers of salmon lived in the river near the sea, but none swam up the river so that people could catch them. Beavers had built a dam and guarded it closely to make sure no salmon went upstream.

Coyote saw that the people were hungry and had no salmon to eat. He told the beaver, "It is not right for you to hold the salmon here. Open the dam and let the fish out." They answered, "We want to keep the salmon for ourselves." Coyote thought of a plan to free the salmon.

He floated down the river in a canoe. When he got close to the dam, Coyote changed himself into a baby and began to cry for food. One of the beavers heard his cries and brought him home. She said to the others, "Look at the baby I found alone in a canoe. Something must have happened to his family." The beavers fed him and put him down to sleep in their house. Coyote watched a beaver take a key from the wall and go out to the dam. Soon, she returned with several large salmon.

When it became dark, Coyote changed himself back into his old self. He took the key from its place on the wall and ran outside. When he unlocked the dam, the trapped fish rushed upstream. Ever since, salmon have been swimming upstream and people have had fish to eat.

Adapted from a Klickitat tale

MAKE A SALMON MASK

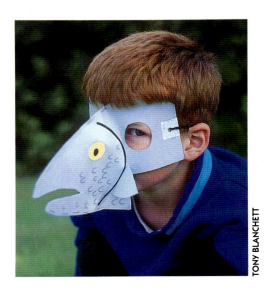

TONY BLANCHETT

2. With the fold at the bottom, measure in from the side, one hand (about 3 inches) wide. Fold over.

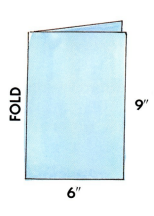

1. Fold a 9×12-inch sheet of construction paper in half.

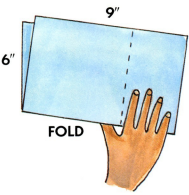

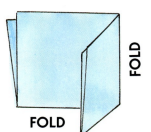

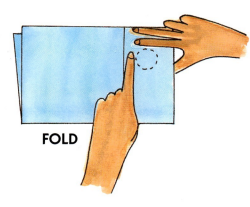

3. Open out and measure for eyeholes on the smaller side, two fingers from the top and one finger in from the side fold.

52

Cut out eyeholes from both thicknesses, making them about two fingers (1¼ inches) wide.

Draw mouth. Cut out mouth; then cut along lines for the head through both thicknesses.

marker. Attach them to the face with glue or tape. Draw gill slit behind the eyes and add scales with crayon or a marker.

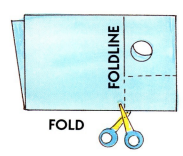

FOLDLINE

FOLD

4. Below the eyeholes, at the bottom edge, cut out a square about three fingers wide. Save the pieces to use for fins.

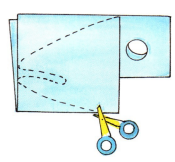

5. Draw a salmon head on the larger side, two curving lines from the top near the eye, to the center of the far side, and from the side to the bottom corner.

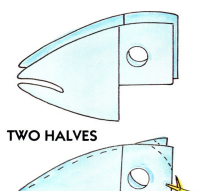

TWO HALVES

STAPLE OR TAPE

6. Staple or tape the two halves of Salmon's head together at the top and bottom, leaving flaps with eyeholes free. Cut off corners near eyeholes.

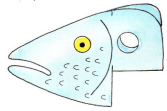

7. Cut two eyes from the yellow scrap. Draw a black pupil inside each yellow eye with black crayon or a

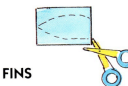

FINS

8. Cut two fins from pieces saved in step 4. Attach fins behind the gills with staples or tape.

9. Wrap a 1 × 3-inch self-adhesive label around each side of the mask behind the eyeholes. Punch holes for ties and attach 12-inch pieces of yarn or string. Stuff a tissue into Salmon's head to give it shape.

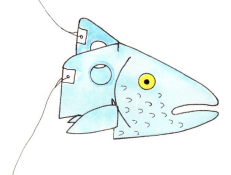

JOY SPURR

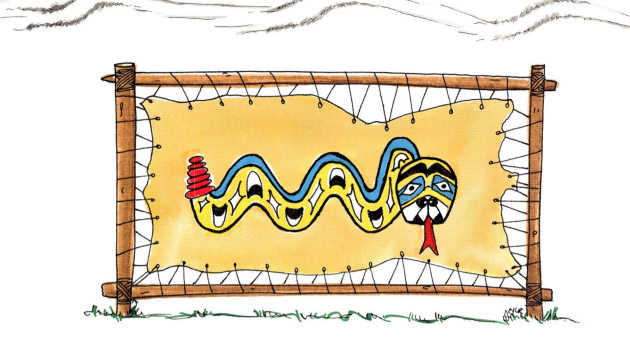

RATTLESNAKE

Rattlesnake and his friends suffered in winter. Each year, the five Snow Brothers who lived in the Sky World covered the villages on both sides of the Cascade Mountains with deep snow. All the animals—Rattlesnake, Mouse, Frog, the birds, and the bigger creatures—wanted to help destroy the bows the brothers used to send the heavy snows. They planned a trip to the Sky World to do this. Traveling many days on land and in air, they finally arrived in the Sky World.

The first night, Mouse went to the Snows' lodge and chewed up four bows while the brothers slept. When the other animals arrived the next morning, the four brothers without bows fled, and the fifth ran to hide in the far North.

Rattlesnake lost track of time, wriggling into cracks and holes near the Snow Brothers' former home, looking for useful things to bring back. When his friends gathered to return home, no one could find him. For many days, Rattlesnake was lost in the Sky World. He finally found his way back down to Earth, but he landed east of the Cascade Mountains. He has never come back over the mountains to the West.

Adapted from a Chehalis tale

MAKE A RATTLESNAKE MASK

Wear Rattlesnake's mask high on the face. Listen for the rattle when Rattlesnake's head moves.

Supplies

- sheet of 9×12-inch tan construction paper
- half sheet of 9×12-inch yellow construction paper
- small piece of white paper for fangs
- small strip of red paper for tongue
- a few kernels of popcorn for rattle
- small scrap of notebook paper about 3×4 inches

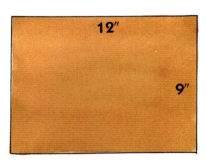

1. Bend a 9×12-inch sheet of tan construction paper into a wide tube. Make the rear opening

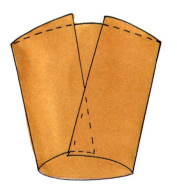

slightly larger than the front opening. Staple overlapping corners together.

EYES

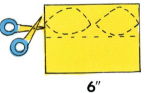

4½″
6″

2. Cut almond-shaped eyes from a 2×6-inch strip of yellow paper. Use a crayon or marker to color in a black pupil. Save the rest of the yellow paper for step 4.

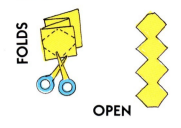

FOLDS

OPEN

RATTLE

3. Attach eyes to the top side of the tube about four fingers back from the smaller open end with staples, tape, or glue. Outline the eyes at the top with black crayon or a marker. Cut the fangs from white paper and the forked tongue from red paper. Attach them at the front of the mouth. Use crayon to color in nostrils and heat pits at the side of the head.

strip of the yellow paper. Fold the strip back and forth on itself, like a fan, and cut a diamond shape through all thicknesses. Be careful not to cut the diamond into a sharp point on the folds, or the diamonds will not stay connected to each other.

6. For Rattlesnake's rattle, roll the piece of notebook paper into a tube and tape the edge. Fold the bottom up about one finger wide, and staple or tape together tightly. Add a few kernels of popcorn, then fold over, and tape or staple the top closed. Attach the rattle to the inside of the mask at the rear, near the bottom so that it doesn't show.

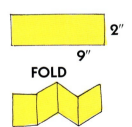

2"

9"

FOLD

4. Cut a diamond-shaped pattern from a 2×9-inch

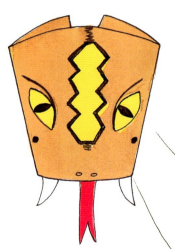

5. Open out and attach the diamond pattern to the Rattlesnake's face and back with tape or glue. Outline with a black or brown crayon or marker.

7. Wrap 1×3-inch self-adhesive label around each side at the lower back of the mask. Punch holes for ties and attach 12-inch pieces of yarn or string.

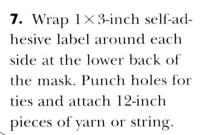

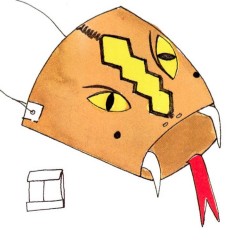

JOY SPURR

OWL

A long time ago, a young woman tended a pot of simmering herring. Her mother-in-law came to visit and said, "That smells good, daughter. What are you cooking?" Not wanting to share the food, the woman answered crossly, "Nothing—only clams." The older person responded, "I'm hungry. May I have a few to eat?" Then the selfish one reached into the pot, but instead of fish, she picked out a steaming rock and dropped it into the old woman's hand. People in the village heard about this rude and selfish behavior and stayed away.

The next day, the young woman went to the water's edge to collect more herring. When she shouted for help to carry her heavy basket of fish, no one paid any attention. She screamed louder and longer, but still the villagers ignored her. She waved her arms up and down and her voice became shrill and hoarse. No one came. Slowly, the selfish woman began looking and sounding more and more like a screech owl—until, at last, she became one.

Now, on dark, quiet nights in the forest, you'll hear her call, "Who, who, who, who-o-o-o-o-o-o." That's to remind us of what can happen to people when they are selfish.

Adapted from a Tlingit transformation tale

MAKE AN OWL MASK

TONY BLANCHETT

Supplies

- sheet of 9×12-inch brown construction paper
- a few dark feathers, if available

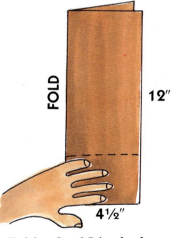

FOLD

12″

4½″

1. Fold a 9×12-inch sheet of brown construction paper in half. Cut about 3 inches off the bottom edge (a piece about four fingers wide).

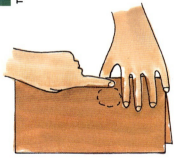

2. Mark the position of the eyeholes using three fingers to measure down from the top edge and one finger in from the fold.

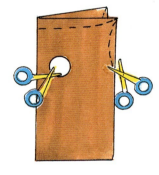

3. Cut eyeholes from both thicknesses, making them about two fingers (1¼ inches) wide. With paper still folded, cut top corners, and along the top edge to make ear tufts on the head.

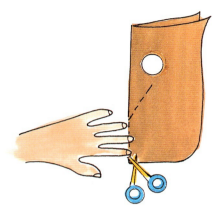

tape to make the beak stand out from Owl's face.

4. For a beak, make a cut along the lower edge of the fold about three fingers long, connecting it to a slash toward the back edge of the eyehole. (Do not cut into the eyehole.) Round the bottom corners of the face.

6. With crayon or marker, draw circles around eyeholes. Make V-shaped marks with crayon or scissors for feathers.

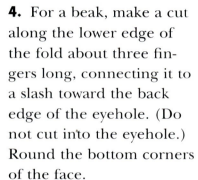

OVERLAP

5. Open up. Overlap corner A over B. Staple or

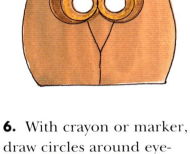

7. If available, add a few real feathers to the face near the eyes.

8. Wrap a 1×3-inch self-adhesive label around each side of the mask. Punch holes for ties and attach 12-inch pieces of yarn or string.

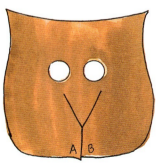

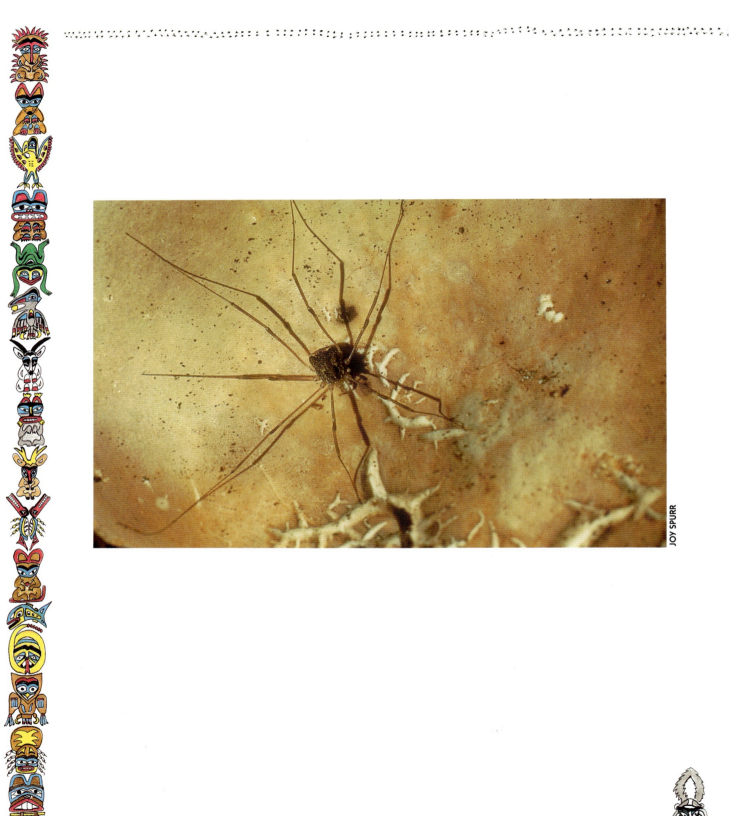

JOY SPURR

SPIDER

In the early days, Spider was a handsome fellow with a well-shaped body who enjoyed a smoky fire. All the young girls wanted to marry him because of his good looks and skill as a hunter, but they could not bear to sit with him in his smoke-filled lodge. Spider had been a bachelor for a long time since no one could pass his smoke test.

Spider liked Beaver's daughter and she wanted to be his wife. As with the other girls, while they visited, smoke clouded the room. Spider waited for her to run outside, coughing like the others and failing his smoke test, but she did not seem bothered. The air thickened and the room darkened. Not able to see her, Spider worried when his young friend did not answer him.

He shuffled around in the darkness, swinging his muscular arms and kicking the floor ahead of him with powerful legs, while trying to find her. When he accidentally struck Beaver's daughter with great force, she grabbed his leg. She pulled it with all her might, and Spider's leg grew longer and thinner, and his body smaller. Then, she did the same thing with his other limbs to even him out. Although he never lost his skill as a hunter, Spider, today, is not handsome. He still has a small, odd-shaped body and long, thin legs.

Adapted from an eastern Washington plateau tribal tale

MAKE A SPIDER MASK

TONY BLANCHETT

Supplies

- 2 sheets of 9×12-inch brown construction paper
- sheet of 9×12-inch yellow construction paper

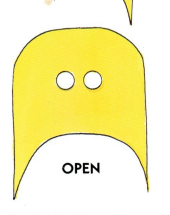

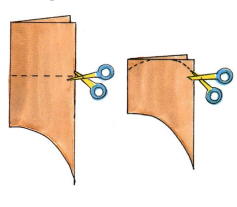

Cut out eyeholes from both thicknesses, making them about two fingers (1¼ inches) wide. Round the outside top corners and open out.

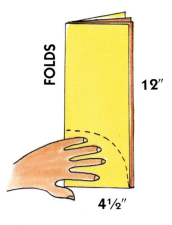

FOLDS

12″

4½″

OPEN

1. For Spider's head, fold together brown and yellow 9×12-inch sheets of construction paper. Starting about four fingers up from the bottom, cut on a curving line from the fold to the outside corner.

2. On the yellow piece, mark the position of the eyeholes using three fingers to measure down from the top edge and one finger in from the fold.

3. Cut the brown piece in half. Save the upper section to use for legs. Round the top corners of the bottom half.

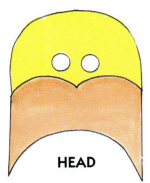

HEAD

Open out and lay the brown strip over the lower half of the yellow piece. Staple, glue, or tape together.

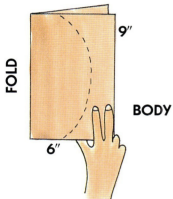

FOLD 9″ 6″ **BODY**

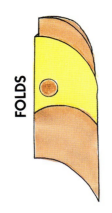

FOLDS

body so that the body shows above the face. Draw round eyeholes with pencil and cut them out of the

tach with glue or tape. Add extra eyes and hair with a crayon or marker.

4. For Spider's body, fold the second brown 9 × 12-inch sheet of construction paper in half. Cut the outside into a gentle curve about two fingers from the edge.

5. To put Spider's head and body together, place the folded yellow and brown face over the brown

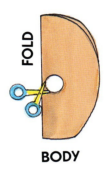

FOLD **BODY**

body section. Open the pieces and staple, tape, or glue in place, making sure eyeholes line up in both pieces.

6. Using the half piece of brown paper saved from the lower head in step 3, cut out eight legs and at-

7. Wrap a 1 × 3-inch self-adhesive label around each side of the mask near the eyes. Punch holes for ties and attach 12-inch pieces of yarn or string.

JOY SPURR

BEAVER

The Pine Trees kept fire for themselves. They would not share it with the Animal People. One day, Beaver saw the Pine Trees meet near the Grande Ronde River. He hid and watched as the Pine Trees stood by the river and warmed themselves at a big bonfire. Shivering, he decided to get the fire. Then Beaver and the Animal People could be warm, too.

Beaver waited until night when the Pine Trees, busy with their meeting, forgot to guard the fire. He left his hiding place, ran quickly toward the bonfire, and took several coals. As he turned to go back to the river, a Pine Tree howled, "Look! Beaver has taken some fire. We must catch him! We must not allow our fire to escape!"

Beaver dove into the water, with the Pine Trees close behind. When the Trees almost reached him, he dodged right, then left, creating sharp bends in the river. Beaver swam and swam, until the Pine Trees, not used to running, began to tire. At first, the Trees stopped here and there along the river. Later, great numbers stopped together and a thick forest grew. Out of reach of the Pines, Beaver stored the fire in the wood of many trees along the banks of the river. Thanks to Beaver, even today, whenever the people need fire, they can get it from wood.

Adapted from a Nez Perce tale

MAKE A BEAVER MASK

TONY BLANCHETT

Supplies

- sheet of 9×12-inch brown construction paper
- two 3×3-inch squares of brown paper, cut from bottom of sheet, for ears
- piece of 1×1-inch black paper for nose
- piece of 2×3-inch white paper for teeth

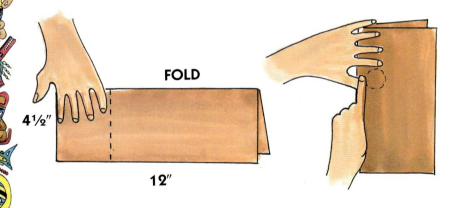

FOLD

4½″

12″

1. Fold a 9×12-inch sheet of brown construction paper in half. Cut off a strip about one hand wide from the bottom edge. Save the strip to make ears.

2. Mark the position of the eyeholes using three fingers to measure down from the top edge and one finger in from the fold.

3. Cut out eyeholes from both thicknesses, making them about two fingers (1¼ inches) wide.

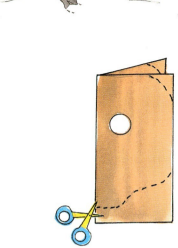

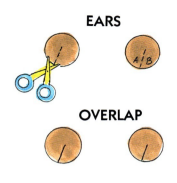

EARS

OVERLAP

4. Cut the top outside corners to make the head rounded. Cut a curving line along the bottom edge to give shape to the lower face.

6. Cut slits from the edge to the center of the ear and nose circles. Overlap edges A and B, and staple or tape them together to make the nose and ears stand out. Attach the ears to the top sides of the head with staples or tape.

the nose. With a crayon or marker, draw a mouth, whisker spots, eyelashes, and fur around the face.

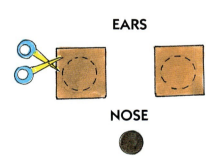

EARS

NOSE

NOSE

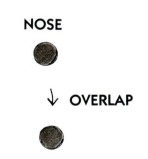

↓ **OVERLAP**

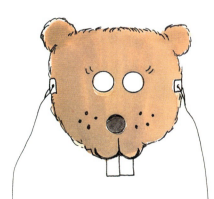

5. For Beaver's ears, cut two circles, three fingers wide, from the saved strip of brown paper. Cut a two-finger-wide circle from black paper for the nose.

7. Cut a slit from the center bottom edge of the face to about three fingers up. Overlap edges A and B and staple or tape to make the face stand out. Attach

8. Cut teeth from white paper and attach. Wrap a 1×3-inch self-adhesive label around the side of the mask near the eyes. Punch holes for ties and attach 12-inch pieces of yarn or string.

JOY SPURR

SKUNK

Badger stayed away from Skunk. He'd heard Skunk possessed great power. One day, as Badger looked for food, he heard a noise and Skunk came out of the brush nearby. Not having time to run, Badger fell to the ground, pretending to be dead. "Now, Skunk won't bother me," he thought.

When Skunk saw Badger's limp body, he picked him up and put him in a sack with some other useful goods. He lifted the heavy bag to his shoulder and walked along, making his noise. He said to himself, "Dead things don't scare me. The only thing I'm afraid of is whistling."

Badger heard Skunk's words from inside the stuffy and cramped sack. He began to whistle. Skunk stopped walking. Badger whistled again. Skunk dropped the sack and ran into the brush. Badger crawled out, took Skunk's goods, and hurried home. Later, he boasted about the trick he'd played on Skunk. "Skunk is not so powerful," he crowed.

Later, Skunk met Badger and some friends. They were joking about Skunk and playing games with his things. Skunk decided to teach them a lesson. He turned around and sprayed them with his musk. As they rolled in the dirt, trying to wipe the smell off their bodies, Skunk took his property back and went on his way, making his noise.

Adapted from a Sanpoil animal tale

MAKE A SKUNK MASK

TONY BLANCHETT

Supplies

- sheet of 9×12-inch black construction paper
- sheet of 9×12-inch white, unlined notebook or computer paper
- 1×1-inch piece of pink paper for nose

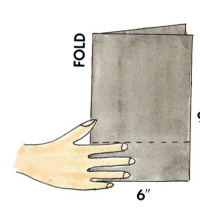

FOLD

9″

6″

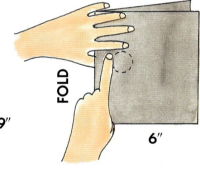

FOLD

6″

7″

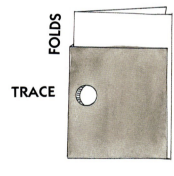

FOLDS

TRACE

1. Fold a 9×12-inch sheet of black construction paper in half. Measure about three fingers up from the bottom and cut off a strip. Save the strip for eyebrows and inside the ears.

2. Mark the position of the eyeholes, using three fingers to measure down from the top edge and one finger in from the fold. Cut out eyeholes from both thicknesses, making them about two fingers (1¼ inches) wide.

3. Fold the white paper as in step 1 above. Lay the folded white paper under the folded black paper so that the white shows above the black. With a pencil, trace the inside edges of both eyeholes on the white piece. Remove the white piece for step 4.

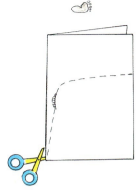

4. On the white piece only, keeping it folded, draw a curving line from one finger above the bottom corner fold to one finger above the eye opening at the open side. Cut. Fold to the inside so that the pencil marks won't show. Save scraps for the outer ears.

FOLD

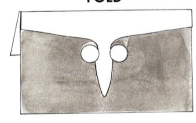

5. Open out the black face piece. Place the white piece over the black, making sure the white does not cover the eyeholes. Fold over excess white at the top. Staple or glue white onto black.

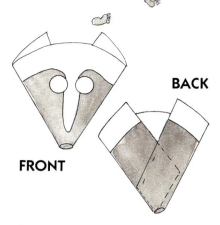

FRONT

BACK

6. Bend the black and white face sheet into a pointed cone shape, leaving a small mouth opening at one end. The other end should be open wide enough to fit over a person's face. Attach the inside corners with staples.

INSIDE EARS   EYEBROWS

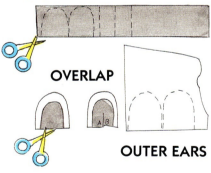

OVERLAP

OUTER EARS

7. Cut the small inside ears from a strip of black paper saved from step 1. Cut the white outer ears from scraps left from step 4. Lay the black ear over the white. Cut a slit into the center and overlap

edges A and B to make the ears stand out. Staple or tape white and black together and attach to the top of the head near the corners.

EYEBROWS

8. Cut eyebrows from the black strip saved from step 1 and step 7. Fringe with scissors and staple or tape in place above the eyes. Cut a nose from pink paper and attach.

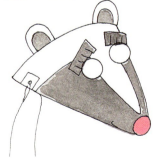

9. Wrap a 1 × 3-inch self-adhesive label around each side of the mask at the bottom corners. Punch holes for ties and attach 12-inch pieces of yarn or string.

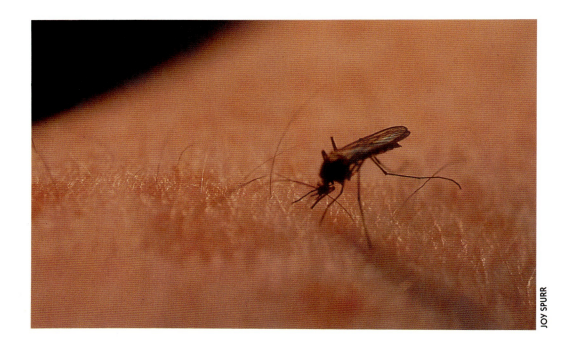

JOY SPURR

MOSQUITO

Giant once lived in the North, feared by everyone because he liked to eat human flesh. Often hunters, searching for game near Giant's camp, failed to return home. A young man whose two older brothers were missing decided to search for Giant. As he walked along the trail, a huge hand reached out from behind a tree, grabbed the youngster, and stuffed him into a sack. Giant took the captive to his lodge, chortling at his good luck, thinking of the tender and delicious meal he would have.

When Giant left to find firewood, the boy struggled out of the bag. Snatching Giant's club, he hid near the doorway. As the monster entered the room, the young man struck him on the head. He found his brothers, and they built a hot, blazing fire. The brothers dragged Giant's massive body into the flames.

Whistling in relief at their narrow escape, the brothers' breath stirred the fire's dying cinders. Ashes rose into the air, becoming a dense cloud of whining mosquitoes. As the men slapped at the pesky insects buzzing in their ears and stinging their flesh, they heard a laughing voice say, "You will never be rid of me. I will always eat you people."

Adapted from a story told by several North Pacific Coast tribes

MAKE A MOSQUITO MASK

TONY BLANCHETT

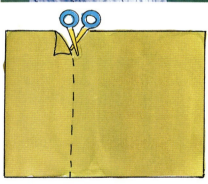

12″

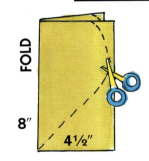

FOLD

9″

8″

4½″

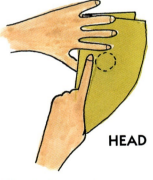

HEAD

1. Cut off about one-third of a 9×12-inch tan sheet of paper, making two pieces, 4×9 inches and 8 ×9 inches. Save the smaller piece for Mosquito's abdomen (rear body part).

2. For Mosquito's face and head, fold the larger piece in half. Cut off the top outside corners. Cut at a slant from the top outside edge to the bottom of the fold, rounding off all sharp points. Save scraps to use for mouth parts and antennae.

3. Mark the position of the eyeholes using three fingers to measure down from the top edge and one finger in from the fold. Cut out eyeholes from both thicknesses, making them about two fingers (1¼ inches) wide.

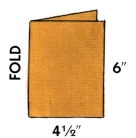

FOLD

6"

4½"

THORAX

4. For Mosquito's thorax (middle body), fold the brown half sheet in two.

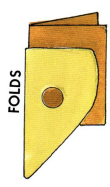

FOLDS

5. To put the face and thorax together, lay the tan face piece over the brown body piece with folds together, so that the face covers more than half of the body. Trace the outline of the eyeholes onto

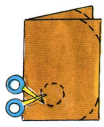

the body. Cut out eyeholes in the body, and round the outside corners. Staple, tape, or glue the face to the body, lining up eyeholes.

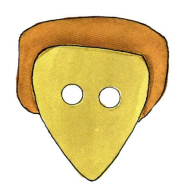

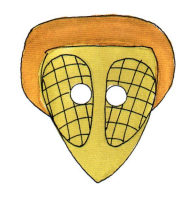

6. Draw large insect eyes around the eyeholes. Mosquito's eyes should cover about half of the face area. Draw crossing lines to look like an insect's compound eyes.

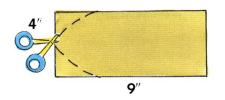

4"

9"

ABDOMEN

7. For Mosquito's abdomen, use the smaller strip of tan paper saved from step 1 and round the corners at one end. Attach this strip to the top of the face and thorax piece with staples, tape, or glue. Add stripes with crayon or marker to the abdomen that look like body segments.

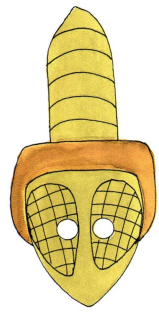

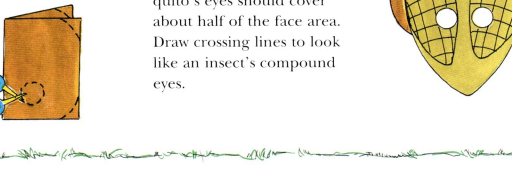

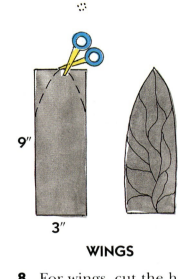

9″

3″

WINGS

8. For wings, cut the half sheet of gray paper in half. Cut one end of each piece to a gentle point. Draw lines with crayon or marker to look like wing veins. Attach wings near the top side of the body. Six legs can be added to the body also, if desired.

9. For mouth and antennae (feelers), use scraps saved from the face in step 2, cut into four thin strips. Use crayon or marker to give a hairy look on the edges. Attach slightly shorter strips at the sides of the mouth and longer ones to the head.

10. For Mosquito's proboscis (piercing mouth part), cut a thin strip from black paper about 6 inches long, and attach it with tape or glue to the center of the mouth.

11. Wrap a 1×3-inch self-adhesive label around the side of the mask near the eyes, below the wings. Punch holes for ties and attach 12-inch pieces of yarn or string.

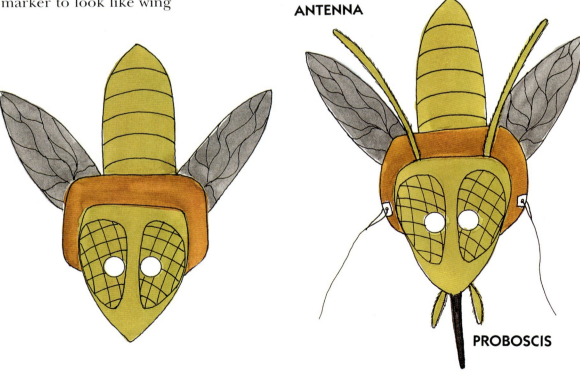

ANTENNA

PROBOSCIS

INDEX

TONY BLANCHETT

(First then second row, left to right)
The children behind the masks are Alex Rutherford, Sandra
Washington, Amanda Perkins, Ian Rutherford, and Emily Mitchell.